An Inquisitive Soul

Jyoti Juneja

BookLeaf Publishing

India | USA | UK

Presentation by *BookLeaf Publishing*

Web: www.bookleafpub.com

E-mail: info@bookleafpub.com

ISBN: 9789360940133

First edition 2024

To the God residing in the hearts of every living being.

Om Tat Sat

ACKNOWLEDGEMENT

I am deeply grateful to those who have supported and inspired me throughout the journey of creating this poetry collection.

First and foremost, I extend my heartfelt gratitude to my family for their unwavering encouragement. Their love and support have been my guiding light.

I'd like to thank the Almighty Lord, my teachers, my friends, classmates, colleagues and admirers for your invaluable feedback, inspiration, support and encouragement. Your insights and encouragement have enriched my creative process and inspired me to push the boundaries.

I express my gratitude to the muses—the moments of beauty, pain, and wonder that have sparked the verses within these pages.

Thank you from the bottom of my heart.

Jyoti Juneja

PREFACE

To all the Inquisitive Souls out there,

"The treasure lies in the depths of the heart and
the whispers of the soul."

UNEXPLORED

I may lie beyond your sight,
An undelved treasure,
Unexplored, but still in delight.

You turned a blind eye,
Doesn't imply I don't exist.
I'm just a far cry,
Dern in the rear of mysterious mist.

But I'm unconcealable for
The Expert's eyes.
Waiting for the one, who can
Softly scrutinize.

"A gem does not seek its possessor; it is the
seekers who discover the gem."

— A Sanskrit Proverb

In the pages that follow, will take you on a journey of discovery, where gems (lessons) of life are waiting to be discovered by those who dare to seek them. In the realm of poetry, "An Inquisitive Soul" encompasses the heartfelt emotions, struggle, pain, perseverance, hope and a search for purpose. It invites you to become a seeker, to delve into the depths of the human experience, and to uncover the hidden gems that sparkle within.

As you read this book, allow yourself to immerse completely in the different realm, become a seeker, opening your mind and heart to the possibility of discovery. For those who seek may find their treasure. Let's embark on the journey of exploration, armed with curiosity, courage, and compassion.

May "An Inquisitive Soul" serve as a guide on your quest for truth, a companion on your journey of self-discovery, and a reminder that within each of us lies a treasure waiting to be found.

With heartfelt gratitude,

Jyoti Juneja

Visit to The Wiz World

I was teleported through a mirror.
I was thrilled, and a bit infused with terror.
It was paradoxical, It was absurd—
I found myself in the World of Wizard.

There I saw Wiz Academic University.
No one knows—it was fallacious or reality!
It seemed like a mickle castle with a cloudy
base,
In which I found a spiral staircase.

I thought it was just a dream.
To confirm, I pinched myself and also screamed,
But it was truly a fantasy world,
Whose mystery was quite curled.

I also participated in the Annual Besom Riding
Race.
I tried to ride it with some pace.
Had fun, but stood last!
Then, from University, I heard a BLAST!

In time equals to a blink of an eye,
I found myself in a room with a wiz saying,
"Goodbye!"

He pushed me into a purplish-sapphire hole.
My sweet dream, by him, had been stolen.

When I awoke, found myself on my bed.
The autumn season came, dreamy leaves were
shed.
Since then, I've never reached there again.
Still waiting for the showers of the dreamy rain.

The Moon

Darkness all around,
Storms in my heart.
Don't go! —My heart yelled.
Stay with me, please.
Wrap me in your arms,
As I feel out of harm's way.

Be with me.
Stars are here,
Sparkling and twinkling,
The diamonds of the sky.
All accompanying the Solitary Moon,
While the rise of the Dynasty of Dark.

Look into my eyes.
Look into my soul.
See what I don't speak,
See what the words can't express.
The scars... The joy...
The unsaid feelings...

Alas! Nothing to say at all
As you made up your mind.
Awkward silences all around...
That night, I was the Moon,

Surrounded by the stars,
Still so lonely.

A Lotus Bud

The legend of a lotus bud,
Originated in the muddy mud.
When ordinary gave birth to extraordinary,
She was wistful for being solitary.

Fragile like touch-me-not,
Unaware of nature's gift, she has got.
Still mourning for inimitable grace
For what she'll earn world's praise.

Mud belittles the bud for being queer,
Unknown of being prominent 'cause of that peer.
The little bud confronting without any spikes,
With the quality of endurance, that she strikes.

Once bloomed into an endearing flower,
Admired by all, contains alluring powers.
Being sober, still filled with elegance,
Hence freed from mud's mocking menace.

World's appraisal and widen glory,
But it's not the end of the story.
The one who praised, plucked her up.
Smashed her splendor and summoned—
"SUPERB!"

Leeches of Love

Love blossoms as white lily,
Selflessly spreading its sweet smell.
Not expecting any reciprocation,
Others find it difficult to repel.

For love is the essence
To make heaven out of hell.
Residing in your heart,
Listen to that ringing bell.

For the times have changed,
That unconditional love is gone.
Among Leeches of Love
I'm having a hard-time to hone.

Leeches of Love
Don't know how to adore.
Magnifying mistakes, highlighting the flaws.
Nothing to love and everything to abhor.

True love is deeper than the Ocean,
But Leeches love shallow.
Loving the image they have of you,
Leaving you feeling hollow.

Leeches' love can be a poisonous fruit.
So beware of false alarms.
Don't be misguided,
Don't let down your guards.

True love appreciates—
The YOU you are.
Accepting all of you.
Even those scars.

Good Night

Love fades away, sweetheart.
People drift apart.
Be okay with it.
All you need is a quick restart.

Universe is infinite.
Like coal, your soul ignites.
Maybe you're dark,
But that's what fuels your spark.

For it takes bleak
To outshine the streak,
When stars fall out
Raining silver sleeks.

I'm carrying the charm
To cause no harm.
I'm the star dust,
Who needs no darn.

The heart they stole was never theirs.
They tried to mend,
Which needed no repairs.
Now I'm reflecting upon it with a glare.

For the pain as deep as black hole,
There's no one around to console.
Some fights are fought within.
Set oneself free on parole.

Some are not worth fighting for.
Averse feeding their ego store.
Let go... Just let it go!
Like a ship leaves ashore.

It's time to take a high-rise flight.
No need to mourn over the plight.
Some blessings are showered in disguise.
Time to sleep... Have a good night!

Bigheadedness

A hard, bigheaded piece of rock,
Got birth from mountain stock.
Brags always about his works—
"I can cause bleeding on collision jerks!"

Destiny intended to teach him lesson,
Got allowance from world's mason.
Made Sunlight, Water and Wind
To rupture his attitude of sting.

The miraculous fused effort they made
As efficient as Ace of Spade.
The snobbishness shriveled into powder
For his existence, none bother.

Never permit superciliousness to rule,
It will mend you to a slacken fool.

Beauty and The Beast

Where there's a Beauty,
There's a Beast.
Loosen slack on virtues,
Who considers her as a feast.

Enchanted by her beauty,
Salivating like a hungry hound.
Her beauty becomes her curse,
When he crosses the bound.

For Beauty is the bait,
Like a fish surrounded by crocodiles.
No matter where she goes,
They'll smell it from the miles.

The beauty they see—
Flesh and blood.
Impaired by vice,
Having hearts of mud.

True beauty is to be kind,
To be humane and divine.
Like a tree offering fruits,
Never saying — "Tis mine!"

Love is innocent,
Love is pure.
Like a Rose spreading fragrance
With no intentions to allure.

Beauty is to witness,
And never to snatch away.
Don't be so selfish,
Keep your filthy intentions at bay.

There's Beauty and the Beast
In each one of us.
Choose wisely—
Who you wanna be, thus.

Lost

Life is a muddled maze.
To be lost is to discover.
The course may be painted with haze.
Keep wandering like a rover.

Here everyone is combating their own battle,
Which seems never ending.
Running after grass like cattle,
Still feeling something's pending.

Nights and days, and nights again!
This is how it goes on...
Life is pleasure-and-pain,
Like a water stream, it flows on...

Here everyone is lost.
Some after worldly possession.
Dreamy eyes dwell in utopia the most.
Lover lost in the eyes of the beloved with
passion.

But if you realize—You're lost,
It turns out to be a turning point.
Battle with oneself—all it costs,
The discovery of oneself—the destiny appoints.

Lost can be an enchanting place
For those lost in self-discovery.
They rise above the worldly haze,
To know the divine—The Universal Mystery!

Amidst Haze

The world's wolf-like eyes staring.
Amidst forests, their eyes are glaring.
Looking up for the prey.
Step inside, don't roam astray!

When the Sun is down,
At the outskirts of the town,
Wolves take over the place.
Don't take a step in a haze!

As the Sun comes up in the East,
Haze blows off along with the beasts.
The right person emerges to rescue,
That changes the entire picturesque.

But, Beware of friendly-foul-frenemies!
Worst of all the enemies.
Wolf wearing sheep's clothing,
Aiming steadily and smothering.

May God shield us from the evils,
Bestow us strength against the perils.
For God is the only Guiding Light,
When Ray of Hope is out of sight.

A refuge that soothes the soul,
Like a diamond amidst the coal.
Adversity turns to blessing in disguise,
Wiser you become, as you realise.

History Lessons

Layers of the Past piled up
Beholding the history,
Lying beneath an off the beaten track,
Covered in mist and an eerie of Mystery.

Past paved a path to the present,
Nurturing the future with knowledge.
Passing on the values and culture
Something that we must acknowledge.

Perfection is a myth.
There are no perfect stories.
What's done and dusted proclaims—
The failure leads to glories.

History tells an ideal tale,
Engraved on the stones of past.
Lot to learn from mistakes
From the people that didn't last.

What is present,
Will be a history tomorrow.
Time shall pass, and only
Lessons will remain to be borrowed.

Four Walls

These Four Walls cannot confine me.
Opinions of the World cannot define me.
I've fire in my eyes, watch your furnace.
Enough is Enough! Can I have my Solace?

These Four Walls don't know Who am I?
I'm Someone, born to touch the Sky.
You can't cage a bird, having urge to fly.
It's my life! Your rules? Why should I comply?

Listen Four Walls! I live on my terms.
My Life shouldn't be one of your concerns.
Yeah, You fortify from potential dangers.
Who are you? One of the Avengers?

Let me go! Let me chase my destiny.
Let me follow my heart's symphony.

Heart's Scream

It's all set up.
Come on! Get up!
Another new day,
Sun's up! Frightening the fog and mist away.

A new day! But the same old story.
Blemished fame and no Golden Glory.
Another new day,
Yet my mind still stuck in history.

Day passes by and Moon comes up.
Sleepless nights that keeps me up.
Never ending loop of thoughts engulf me.
Bit by bit, I'm losing it all and my Heart pleads.

Troop of Thoughts pointing Spears at me,
That saddens my Heart, replacing the glee.
Sounds like a song!
But it's actually my Heart's scream.

What's shattered, can't be undone.
All the efforts proved to be mundane.
"Let bygones be bygones." —
Easily said than being done.

Feeling stuck, plotting my escape.
Fighting the odds, concealed under drape.
Hardest battles are fought within.
Mind can be a difficult place to live in.

Crippled

You want me to be Red!?
Great! I'll be Red.
You want me to be Blue!?
Awesome! I'll be Blue.
No one wondered—
What God made me to be.
They all wish to see...
What they want to see.
But, What about me?
Now I'm lost between Reds and Blues.
Wondering the colour of my hues.
Will I ever find it!? God only knows.
Marked with resentments as cold as Snow.
Crippled by Expectations,
The ones were my aspirations.
I question —What I truly desire?
Is there anything that I admire?
Lost myself while attaining the bars,
All I'm having is deep dark scars.
Agony choking me to death,
Deepening scars with every breath.

Having Hope

Heart's deepest desire—
Unwind your wings
And fly as far as you can!
Break the Bars
And your Freedom Ban!

Fight! Fight! Fight!
Steal everything you can!
No more restrictions,
Feel the freeness, Baby!
It's life! Not a set of fictions!

Stop! Stop! Stop!
What are you doing!?
Wait for a while!
Something is missing, Baby!
Oh! You forgot your smile!

Think! Think! Think!
Have got nothing to lose,
Just few pieces of hammered heart!
In the world, which is frozen,
How can I rejuvenate and restart!?

Oh my dear! Don't think much!

Have faith! Perseverance pays!
It's hope that gleams in your eyes!
Seasons may favor,
If you dare to walk few extra miles!

Blues

Encircled by illusions, drifting in its trap.
Life is a maze! And everything is crap!
Perplexed by its frame, I usually wonder—
"Why am I here?"—Having a heart full of
thunder.

This mind-altering phase, I'm going through.
Incognizant, to overcome the blues.
Yelling for aid, nobody's listening to.
Being my own Hero, I'm confronting too.

Reaching the horizon, I could see.
Not everything is— as it appears to be.
All preconceived notions washed away.
I'm here, contemplating at the bay.

I may or may not have a reason to be...
I'm attempting to solve life's mystery.

Striving to Outshine

Deep down I feel dead inside.
Guess what!? Nobody gives a damn!
No one's there to stay beside.
Shut them out. Try not to lose the calm.

Seek solace in solitude.
Dig deeper, deeper into the life!
Let's put Life mode on "Reviewed"!
Why it cuts like a knife?

A diamond undergoes cutting,
Just to outshine.
Perhaps it's inevitable to confront blues,
To get in the vicinity of the Divine.

No one's going to make it alive.
Do find out what you really strive.

Blessing in Disguise

I am the Sun.
Like me, there's none.
For I may not know the gloom
As I make the flowers bloom.
All I emit is light,
Casting shadows amidst the bright.
Sometimes it gets lonely
As I brighten up the celestials solely.

"Yes, Yes.", the Moon reckoned,
Still feeling being shunned.
" I do understand your plight.
You're brilliant and ignite.
You get all the limelight
And I get to wait till it's night."

Despite being an gem of the night,
Moon is saddened, feeling no delight.
Dependent on the Sun for its glaze,
As the Sun is fierce with his blaze.

Feeling like an outcast,
Both sinking in the Sea of Sorrows.
Moping as if there's no tomorrow.

God showered them with blessings,
With which, they both were messing.
For they might not know their offerings.
It's their minds that require conquering.

They are perfect with imperfections.
No need for further corrections.
For God knows what's best for us,
Hence, no need to make a fuss.

Art by Almighty

This world is a piece of art,
Filled with fascination.
Shaded with lights and dark,
Incredible, beyond imagination!

Dipped in vibrant emotions
From God's colour palette.
Like ravishing roses,
Life blooming in every facet.

Within the depths of Oceans
The God's treasure withheld.
The Waves whispering
At the shores, to tell.

Silver shimmering threads
Emitted by Stars and Moon.
Sewing the secrets
With darkness and gloom.

Wind howling through the hair,
Carrying aroma along...
Softly caressing cheeks with flair,
Singing a sweet song.

Enchanted by God's grace,
Mesmerized — I feel.
Appreciating the Art by Almighty,
Full of life and zeal.

Delusion

It may not be what it seems,
One assumes, let mind screams.
No perception would be bias-free.
It's all a lie, growing into a delusional tree.

One tells oneself what we believe,
Soothes our hearts or agonize in grief.
The reality will stand still,
Immovable like a mountain hill.

Obscured by granules of sand,
You may need a helping hand.
For the storm so intense,
Distorted vision can no more pretense.

Truth is unshakeable, unlike pretty little lies,
As clear as a mirror, following the stormy skies.
The Truth may taste bitter, but sets you free.
Accept it to find solace from the stress-spree.

Let all delusions dissolve, let there be light.
Just give in to the truth, let there be delight.

Rise Like A Warrior

A treacherous habitation,
Where snarling monsters roam.
Lurking around to eat you up—
Prowl, stalk and groan.

Attempting to belittle your spirit
To crumble you from the core.
Let them rattle, give in to the battle.
They'll be hushed on hearing you ROAR.

Pound back with due actions,
Compel them to bow.
Rise like a warrior.
You're the King—They'll know.

Turn a deaf ear to vilifying voices.
Acknowledge your existence by God's grace.
Rise like a warrior with your poises.
Fight imperfections, let struggles embrace.

Believe thyself! The king at the core.
Lions don't Meow, they only ROAR.

Potential

Adjusting to the world is never easy.
People proclaim as it keeps them busy.
Either you're too lean or too stout.
You just can't say—" Shut your mouth!"

Zillions of people, Zillions of eyes.
Some new meet, some goodbyes.
Different people, different opinions.
Either you're mature or maniac minions.

No matter what you are,
You're still made up of star.
The light that shines within
Will let the change begin.

So slay all your self-doubts.
Just forget about how-abouts.
Let the others do the talking.
Choose a path and keep on walking.

There's no right or wrong.
Listen to your soul & stay strong.
For people mock at complex minds,
Don't let it make you sour like tamarind.

Each fruit has a different taste.
No flower blooms in the haste.
Why compare? Why expect?
Can't we keep aside our dialect?

Yes! The change begins with one.
It can be you, other than none.
Grasp the grip of what you believe.
Inner satisfaction is a better relief.

No matter if you fail or succeed.
Atleast you tried, rumours shall breed.
If intentions are pure,
Then people may allure.

For you shall witness the magic,
That will fade away all that's tragic.
Petty pebbles create ripples in lake.
Stick to the path for heaven's sake.

Single Spark can turn into forest fires.
Don't bother about—who admires.
Even little atoms can blow up the town.
Let them consider you a clown.

Powerful potential that you withhold
Can pave the path amidst the cold.
Be your own furnace, be your light.
It will lead you to ecstatic delight.